Feelings

Sad

Sarah Medina

Illustrated by Jo Brooker

Heinemann Library
Chicago, Illinois

Photo research by Erica Martin
Designed by Jo Malivoire
Printed in China by South China Printing Company Limited

11 10 09 08 07
10 9 8 7 6 5 4 3 2 1

Library of Congress Cataloging-in-Publication Data
Medina, Sarah, 1960-
  Sad / Sarah Medina.
      p. cm. -- (Feelings)
  Includes bibliographical references and index.
  ISBN-13: 978-1-4034-9293-7 (hardcover)
  ISBN-10: 1-4034-9293-X (hardcover)
  ISBN-13: 978-1-4034-9300-2 (pbk.)
  ISBN-10: 1-4034-9300-6 (pbk.)
  1. Sadness in children--Juvenile literature. I. Title.
  BF723.S15M43 2007
  152.4--dc22

                    2006025132

Acknowledgments
The author and publisher are grateful to the following for permission to reproduce
copyright material: Bananastock p. **22A, D**; Corbis p. **10** (top right); Getty Images/The
Image bank, p. **22C**; Getty Images/photodisc p. **10** (bottom left & bottom right); Getty
Images/Taxi p. **22B**.

Every effort has been made to contact copyright holders of any material reproduced
in this book. Any omissions will be rectified in subsequent printings if notice is given
to the publisher.

Contents

Some words are shown in bold, **like this**. They are explained in the glossary on page 23.

What Is Sadness?

Sadness is a **feeling**. Feelings are something you feel inside. Everyone has different feelings all the time.

happy

angry

sad

When you are sad, you might feel upset. You might cry.

What Happens When I Am Sad?

When you feel sad, you might not want to play or help around the house. You might want to be on your own.

Sadness can make you feel empty inside. You might not feel like eating.

Why Do I Feel Sad?

You might feel sad when people **argue**.

Remember to ask for help and to do things that are fun. Then your sadness will pass quickly.

How Can I Tell If Someone Is Sad?

When people are sad, they might not want to play with you. They might just want to be on their own.

They might tell you to go away.
Remember, it is not your fault. They are
just feeling bad inside.

Can I Help When Someone Is Sad?

You can help people when they feel sad. Be kind to them. Invite them to play with you.

Ask them why they are sad. If they stay sad, ask an adult for help.

Is It Ever Good to Feel Sad?

Remember, everyone feels sad
sometimes. Sadness goes away
after a while.

It is good to learn what to do about sadness. Then you can help yourself and others, too.

What Are These Feelings?

A

B

C

D

Which of these people look happy?

What are the other people feeling?

Look at page 24 to see the answers.

22

Picture Glossary

argue
when people do not agree
and sometimes yell at
each other

cheer up
feel happier

feeling
something that you feel
inside. Sadness is a feeling.

Index

Answers to the questions on page 22

The person in picture C looks happy. The other people could be sad, angry, or jealous.

Note to Parents and Teachers

Reading for information is an important part of a child's literacy development. Learning begins with a question about something. Help children think of themselves as investigators and researchers by encouraging their questions about the world around them. Most chapters in this book begin with a question. Read the question together. Look at the pictures. Talk about what you think the answer might be. Then read the text to find out if your predictions were correct. Think of other questions you could ask about the topic, and discuss where you might find the answers. Assist children in using the picture glossary and the index to practice new vocabulary and research skills.